God's Broken Machine

Poems and Art

by

Michael E. Kelley

First Edition

Little Red Cell Publishing
North Platte, Nebraska, USA

First Edition, 2016, printed and bound in the USA

Book Design: Michael J Linnard, MCSD

1 2 3 4 5 6 7 8 9 10 LSI 22 21 20 19 18 17 16
Set in Zapfino, Trajan Pro and Times New Roman

International Standard Book Number:

Hardbark: ISBN: 978-1-935656-42-5

All poetry and artwork by Michael E. Kelley
Front Cover illustration is titled, "The Rescued" by Michael E. Kelley. It also appears on page 32.

Library of Congress Cataloging-in-Publication Data:

Kelley, Michael E.
 God's Broken Machine: Poems and Art/ by Michael E. Kelley. -- 1st ed.
    p. cm.
  Includes Index.
  ISBN: 978-1-935656-42-5 (pbk. : alk. paper)
  I. Poetry. II. Title.
  PS3623.O664S93 2016
  811'.6--dc22

Little Red Cell Publishing
North Platte, Nebraska, USA
www.littleredcell.com

CONTENTS

INTRODUCTION

God's Broken Machine, is my second book of poetry combined with art. I chose this title because it is what I am, among various other unsavory titles. This book is a collection of my poems, with my art: line drawings, color drawings and paintings. The poems and illustrations depict precious pain, sweet memories, and the multiple identities I have lost along the way.

What you'll find within these pages, are the end results of a bullied and marginalized life. However, I don't blame others for my criminal acts, nor do I beg you to excuse them, and I take full responsibility. Nevertheless I do pray for understanding and forgiveness. Both of which are in short supply.

It is my hope that everyone who picks up this book will read the poems, look at the art, see and feel the loss and somehow find it in their hearts to be kind to those less than themselves In short be compassionate and humane to the person next to you.

Michael E. Kelley,
Massachusetts. January 2016

DEDICATION

Thanks to Ralph C. Hamm III, Big Red & his Flaming Spoon, The Fully Alive Brothers and Kat, but mostly thanks to God for the gift of these talents that help my humanity to survive and Crystal Marie, I love you and miss you

God's
Broken Machine

For My Sister ...

Mary, Mary, what can I share,
Any words I say would not be fair...
Your passing really caught me quite unaware,
When I learned how little people really care.
A lesson that forgiveness is a gift so rare,
Our brothers and sisters love of popularity I don't share...

So from one who's existence others can't bear,
Maybe just a simple knave, to show I care.
Those flowers you loved, in heaven you can wear,
You'll find your rabbit Petey climbing the heavenly stairs.
With our brothers laughter you'll share,
Your Buster will be there, and you won't have a care...

Eileenie...

Sometimes in life,
there are moments that pass,
unnoticed by any, a moment
of kindness to the one of infamy.

A touch of human grace,
fore told of God's embrace,
the notice of unwarranted pain
healing the marks left by the insane.

The memory of your face,
always be held in that broken boys space,
your blessing was never told,
at that moment you acted so bold.

Your kindness, kept humanity's spark from growing cold,
an act of kindness that must be told, before we get too old....

The Top Five of You

The imprint of you still has it's command,
even through times passing sands
Your love of Mr. Purple socks,
really came as no shock

An impish grin you gave to me, when you teasingly
danced to "Give it to me," even Geils would have to smile
And your impression of a Man Eater
could turn any air-conditioner into a heater ...

A smolderin' demand when you heard the sister's slow hand,
Heat that can be felt with twenty years in the can
And when Your Kiss... was a wish to make a crippled man stand
But, for me it will always be the bet of, ambitious

Crystal Marie

Once upon a time, as an opening plea,
I'd use your name in a verse, when you were wee.
It would say, Crystal Marie's as pretty, as pretty, can be.

As you see in this art,
a rare beauty indeed,
This anyone can see

Like your mother before you couldn't see,
the raven haired beauty that she be,
a gift she gave to Crystal Marie,

The art, like the many who've seen
inspired by you, exclaim the same as me,
Crystal Marie's as pretty as pretty can be

Piccasso, Max, Parrish and Christy would agree,
A beauty like your's will set colors free,
Thank you for being Crystal Marie

Rocker Girl

There are moments that say nothing and everything in one look...
    The impish glint of the eye,
    The knowing smile,
    The sassy tousled hair,
    As if you didn't care.

Combinations innocently caught in a sudden glance...
    These are life's lovely gifts,
    Momentary glimpses of stardom,
    Sharing in the Movie,
    The movie of you...

Intertwining of joy, amusement, pride, wonder, and humor
Flow through the pencil and pen,
Sharing talent and honor with vision that's you...

Run Away

One day, oh so long ago,
I played the part,
of a normal Joe,
Always on the go,

no time to take it slow...
A wife, a life, struggle and strife,
all these I remember as I lay awake every night.
Things I'd dreamed would make my life alright.

Memories that don't fade, no matter the passing decades.
Dreams that will never see their final play.
No one knows what to say, when the chance to say
I love you, passes away, always knowing that
we'll never pass this way...

The early morning rain greets this day,
All these words that I could say.
The burden of truth is something to weigh
the price of innocence it would slay,
it's better to run away...

White Goddess

A Texas tornado, from the land of yellow dirt,
You came along when life was nothin' but hurt,
The laughing lady, an incorrigible flirt.
A blonde bombshell in a tight sexy skirt...

For sixteen years, you've shared your tears,
fears, and moments of cheer,
always wishing you could come near.
But, Texas girls don't like the snow, I fear...

Now the moniker of "White Goddess" might seem inane,
In some traditions, that's a literal translation of your name,
Now the title's quite plain, I'm just sayin',
I ain't really that insane, just operatin' on a different plane.

Between us there's been too many a mile,
but knowing you has brought many a smile.
Your Texas accent, my hearts been beguiled,
I got love for you, girl, you know you're my style.

So don't blush, or be modest, when you're called the
"White Goddess," you know that it only means your
name is Michelle...

Closet Case

Don't look too hard at this face,
don't think you can replace
a heart that's an empty space.
You're taken it all away,
there's nothing left here on which to prey...

Go ahead and count my regrets,
held over my head, of mistakes not made yet.
Go ahead and make my sin's bleed,
you forget my debt was your need
for this love was suppose to set us free...

Yes I knew I let you down,
now you won't come around,
your judgements make me the clown,

Take a good look at yourself,
Take away your imagined wealth,
life, love, and memories tossed on a shelf,
this is the hand you dealt...

Control over love, with no room to grow,
passion's measured as reality wouldn't show.
And love for a lady made you glow,
with a husband just for show...

Peace with the Past

I've come here at last,
wondering about peace with my past,
Gordon's words echo around my head,
Reminding me that all I love call me dead.
Sorrow and shame, are the weight of lead...

To believe and to trust,
God, is this really a must?
To forgive and to forget
is for those who have no regret.
Love's always been like any empty room to let,
trust is a losing bet and hope a promise I've not seen yet...

For me to conceive
of a peace to believe,
I have to find a way to relieve,
a dream that will never be...

Peace is a need,
a pray for my soul, not bleed.
Tell me how to believe...
Tell me what to believe...
No seed, no root, no shoot,
all these needs are hard to conceded,
as long as the child inside needs
a place to hide, with no place for peace to abide.

Dusk's Delight

As I looked... the dusk was dancing to my west,
the magic of daylights colorful egress ...
The marvel of mother nature's wonderful paintbrush,
splashes of fiery red, orange, yellow, mystical magenta, and
hints of violet too!!!

Marveling at where the green dissolves to indigo blue,
introducing the night to me and you...

As I stood... the dusk danced to my west,
I knew that I'd been blessed...
In awe of the divine, echoed in my chest,
knowing this moment is how GOD must caress,
calming the soul of life's daily stress...

As I stood... the dusk danced to my west,
knowing nothing,
      wanting nothing,
           passing into nothing...
the moment has come and gone,
it's gift is the night and the coming dawn...
      that rises in the east...

Blind Tears

Heard the tale of a blind man's tears,
Telling a story of sadness, I knew so well.
I heard you're leaving, so just close the door,
I won't be a part of humanity anymore,
no one will be knocking at my door...

Sitting in the darkness,
lingering in the emptiness of ever more,
orphaned by those whom I loved and adored.

I had a daughter once before,
but said I wasn't her father anymore.
Broken by the venom she spat at my door,
and all the dreams shattered on the floor...
but the love still yearns for more.

And what of tales told so well,
one can feel the flames of this living hell,
the blind man tears, a pain deeper than a well...

God's Broken Machine

What was the line, and what did it mean.
Can life really be lived and appear so clean.
This claptrap crap sounds like dream,
But then again I'm just one of God's broken machine's ...

I sit and listen to society's garbage, till I wanna scream.
Sometimes I'm just glad I can't be seen,
as this life seems fit only for the drama queens.
But then again I'm just one of God's broken machine's

War in the Middle East, bombings, killings, teenager's
acting like beasts, seems as if the devil's having a feast,
it's no wonder that Jesus is still on his knees.
But then again I'm just one of God's broken machine's

Doin' my time, penance for my unspeakable crime,
so what I see and say ain't worth one thin dime.
Half of you act like you ain't even human kind.
But then again I'm just one of God's broken machine's ...

Cell phone and tones, you pay your neighbor no mind,
No wonder your children tell you to kiss their behind.
Your wife, or your lover, you just ain't got the time.
It's grime you need to clean, just noise from God's broken machine.

I've Lost

I've lost everything, and everything's lost me,
Looking for the dawn like some lost friend,
I cry out loud, a man with no pride,
I knew I'd reach the end,
Thought I saw a crazy old man.
It was the reflection of the man I'd become...

A wanderer in the dark of night,
looking up at the stars of night,
telling me to hold on tight,
no promises that it would be alright,
grabbing on to those tiny points of light,
hoping with all my might,
just to make it through the night,
just trying to make it to the light,
just prayin', no more reasons to fight,

No more dreams that'll be alright,
No more dreams of earthly fright,
No screams to be right,

I've lost everything, and everything's lost me.
Lost what used to be, and lost what will never be.

Emptiness & I

If I spoke out loud of the sorrows I've known,
of the dark secrets I own, and shame that can't be shown,
emptiness that cannot atone, that cries to be left alone.
Talkin' only reminds me of broken bones...

Emptiness is my savior, because we're two of a kind.
Truth can't savored as the words would make you blind,
and a love is best left behind...

Emptiness knows that terror rules, bullies and jack asses are
considered cool, where secrets are cruel, secrets are fuel,
that cripple and ridicule, creating lands where rage and suicide rule,
human desire, makes you a fool, a discarded stool ...

Emptiness won't speak out loud, lies and hatred that sear to
the bone, knowing no friend or foe to beacon me home,
always broken and alone, wandering afar to places unknown,
carrying some sin that won't be atoned, innocence hidden
where the light can't be shown, emptiness is all that's known.

A mothers unwarranted charges, disparage the youthful flame,
unkind titles that cripple and lame, no value only shame,
never seen as the same, eyes of contempt, sneers of utter disdain,
a haven of hatred and blame, a creep she gave as my name ...

Emptiness never spoke of the scorn of the second born,
word by word the dignity was torn, beatings and betrayals
never mourned, this is how Emptiness's rage was born ...

Silence

Listening to the silence in my soul,
as secrets of my history breathe
a low and mournful song.
Please don't repeat it's refrain
kept locked deep within...

Deep in the depths, sheltered,
memories of rain, days of disdain,
childhood's bitter chains ...

Speaking with the silence,
the soul will come to know
all the creaks and moans,
and the emptiness I've known...

Desire and need, like weeds, so dense
and overgrown, with no place to call home,
just an ache in the bones...

Embrace the silence in my soul,
marvel at thoughts of being whole,
with memories of love and moments I stole,
fleeting movements, nothing to hold...

Dream with the silence in me,
peace is an illusion, flowing free,
like sand on the tips of my hand.

Silence is the sacred part of me,
secrets are the silence, I can never be free ...
from the silence in me...

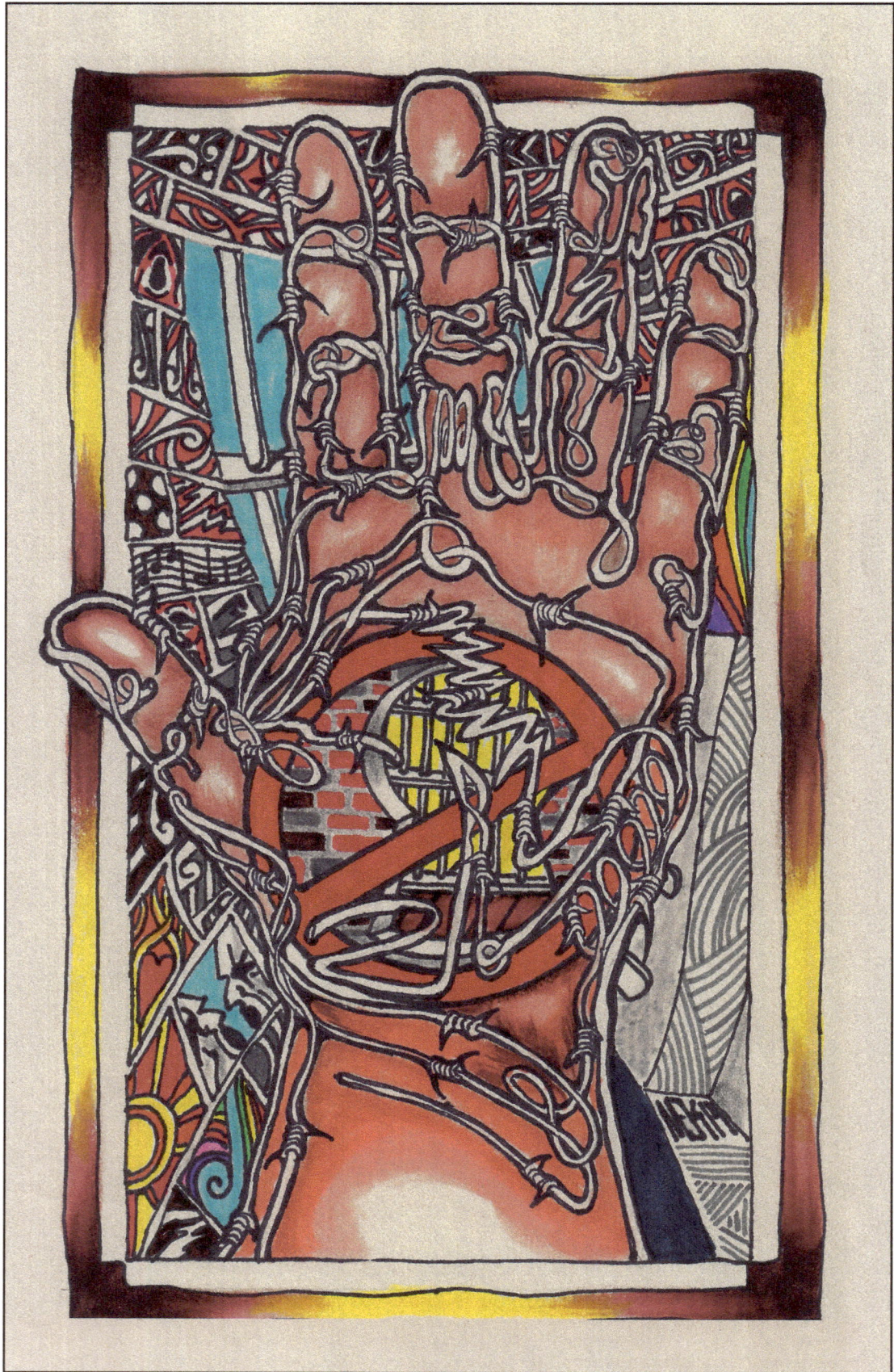

Sounds of Sorrow

Sounds of sorrow sing,
silently stinging deep within,
rendering it's empty echoing din.
Again and again, no beginning, no end,
the notes, the song, a symphony of sin,
this is all that's ever been...

From the darkness to the light,
wiped from the universal list
by the claim, by the name, the mantle of the right.
My name's been taken, no birth, no burial,
so sublime, so mercurial is this curse...

Many is the claim by the sainthood of the right.
Where to begin. I'm the face of original sin.
Never known to fit in.
A lonesome loser can't fit in.
A lonesome loser can never win.
Can't you see I'm no one's kin.
Never wearing truth, having no roots.
Life and love denied by my own shoot.
Life's point has been rendered moot...

A nameless face is a soul deprived of living fame,
and spiritual madness a torturers game.
Political parasites feed on my remains,
siphoning all, till only the beast remain,
Chanting messages of hate and shame...

Redemption denied, accusations of blame,
vengeance, hatred, extinguish life's flame.
Mercy has no place, in justice's name....

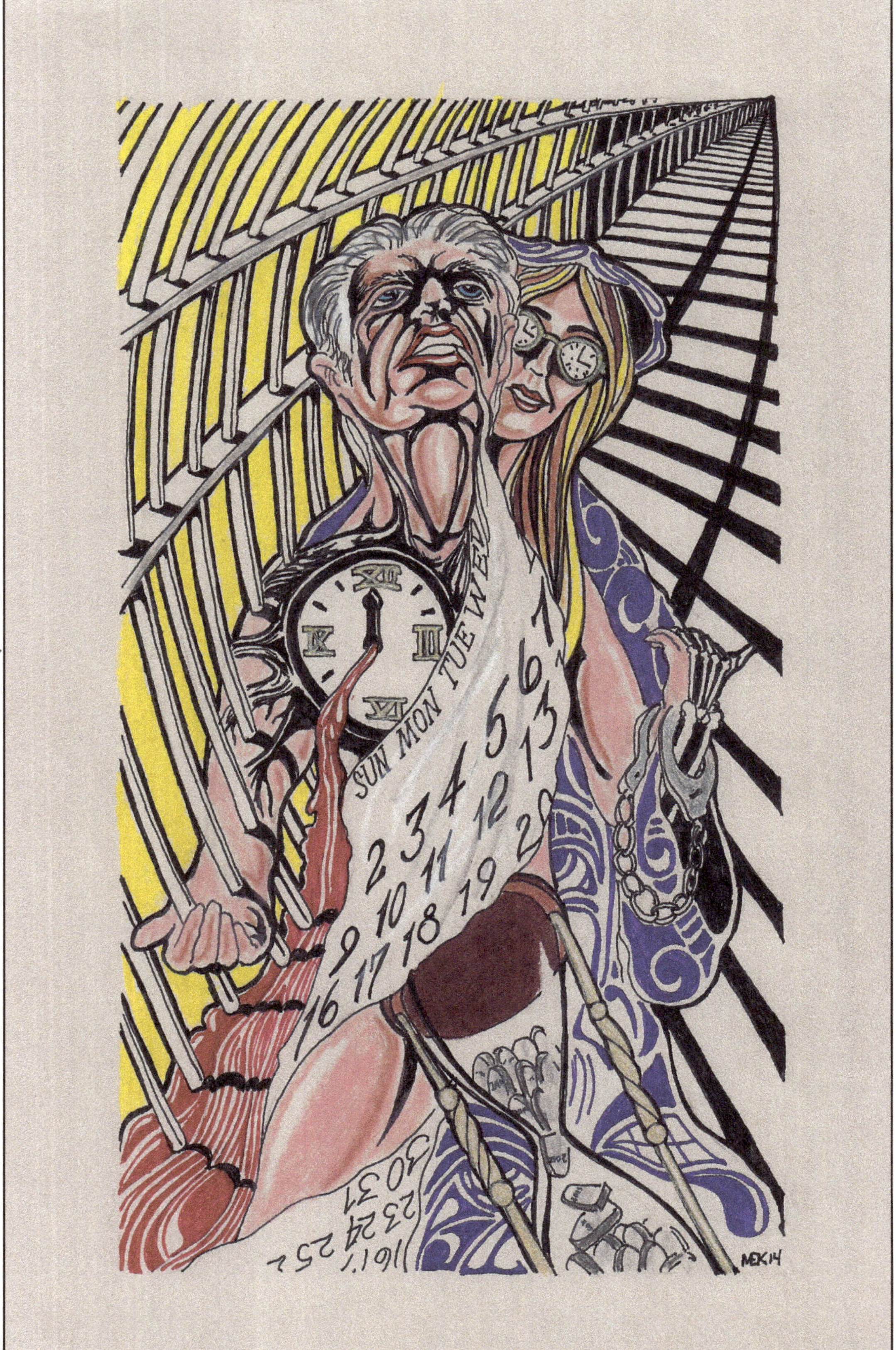
SUN MON TUE WED
MEK 14

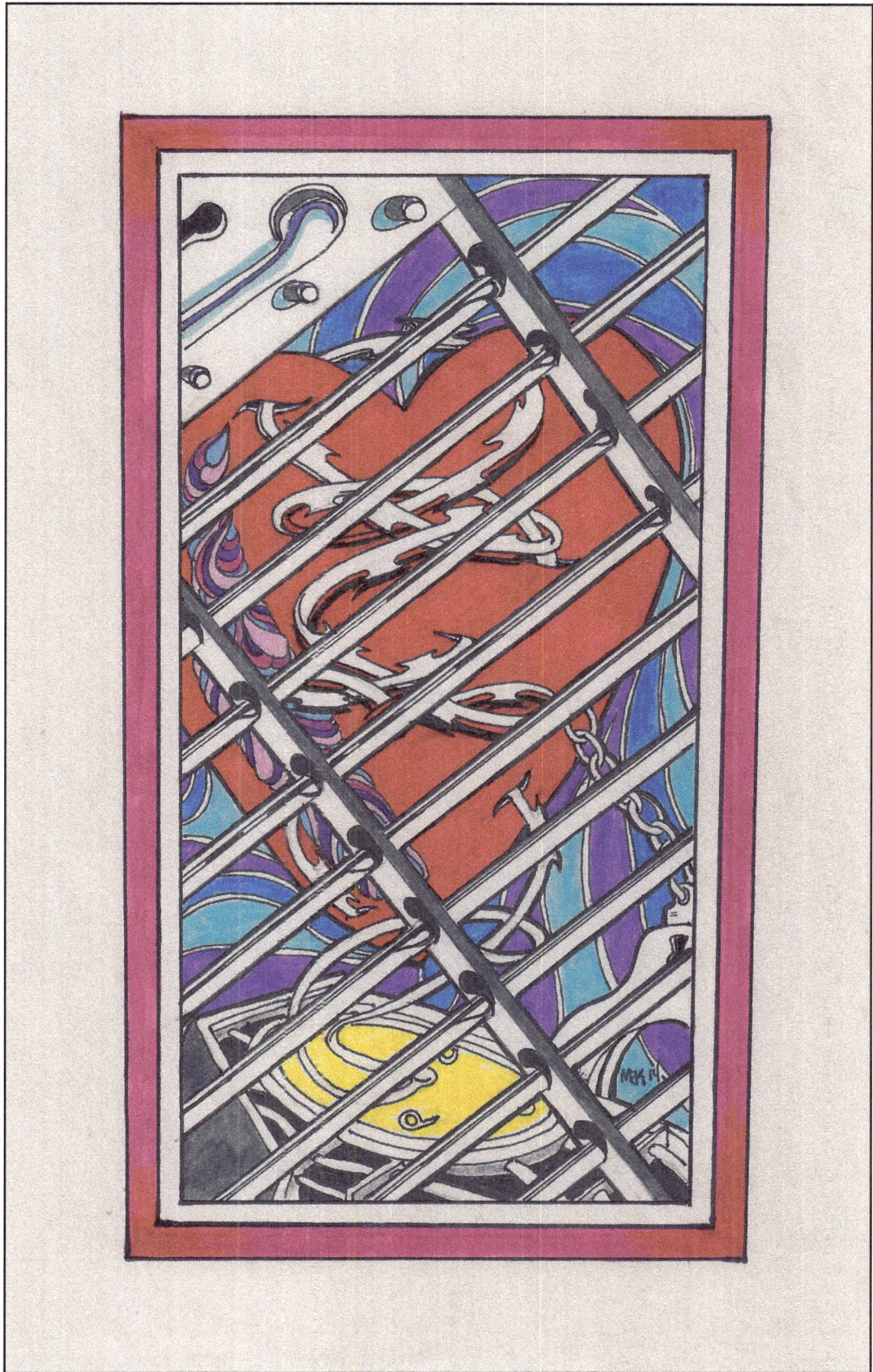

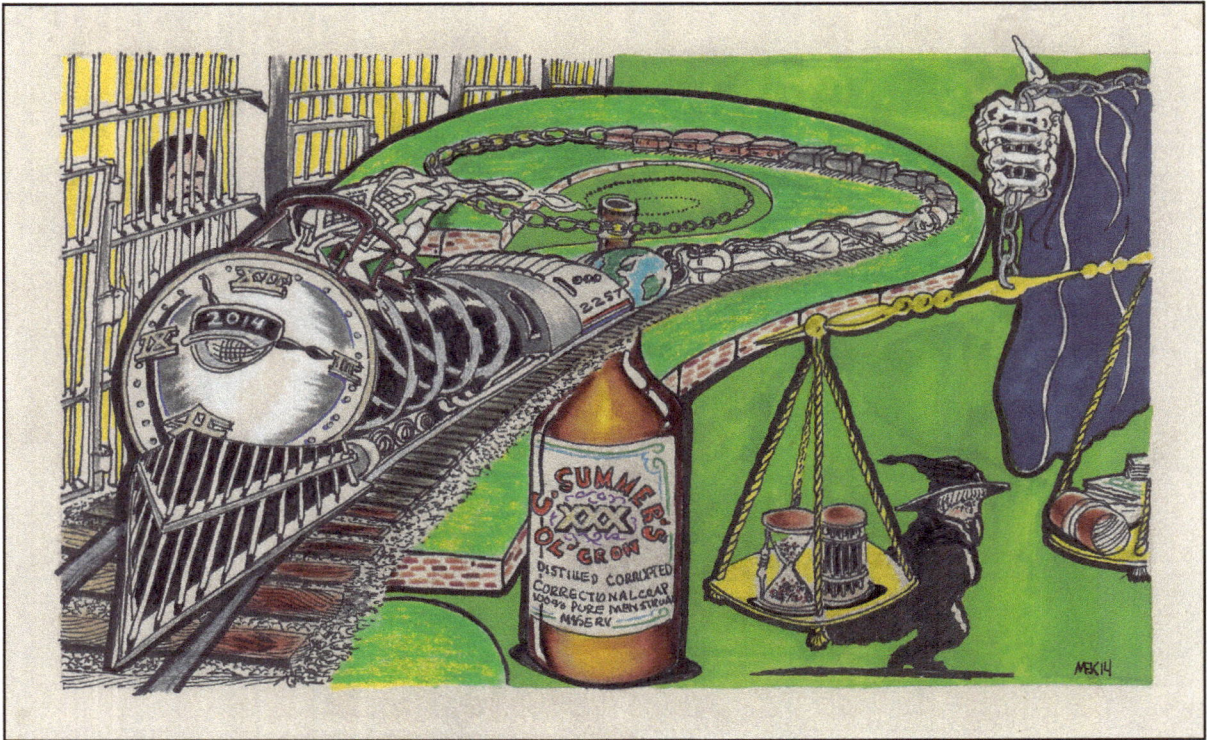

Morning Prayer

Jesus buddy, Ol' pal,
can ya stop and sit awhile,
can ya hear my prayers,
can ya hear my cares.
I know my words ain't got flare,
But, I could use a friend to share,
the miles have begun to show the wear.

There's been many a lonely mile,
It's really tough to muster up a simple smile,
I wonder if you're amused, bemused,
or just plain bored...

Hearin' me beggin' each time I knock on your door...

Hearin' these frantic pleas,
as I place on bended knees,
for peace, for release from past deeds,
please heal this bent, broken reed...

You know I've often wondered how I came to be,
needing help like never before,
tired of sittin' outside life's closed door,

A misfit, a jerk, shame covers me like dirt.
Wandered and pondered, don't like what I see.
Can ya tell me, is this all I'll ever be,
does salvation include people like me.
I understand why humanity smirks,
just one of life's unanswered quirks...

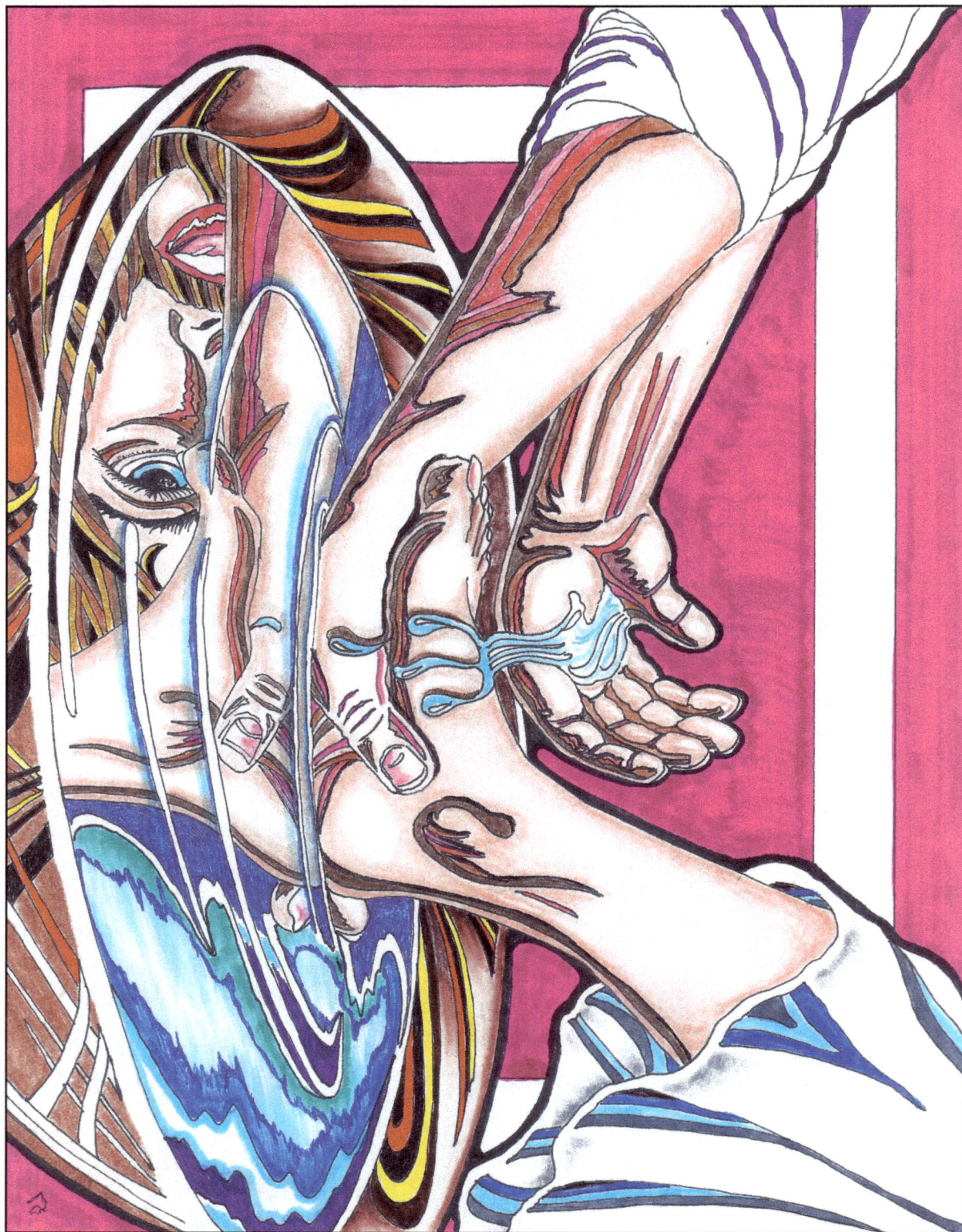

Washing of the Feet

A place so far from the human heart you held,
worn, torn, ravages born, from the pilgrim's sojourn...
Water's graced by your healing hand,
a lesson, a blessing, by the leader of the band...
A moment more than Peter could understand,
yet he simply submitted to the master's plan...
It is, it was, more than just the master washing
a servant's foot, love's been shown, simply put,
a teaching, we must own, to show how salvation grows...
Who's been humbled? What is meek? Jesus washed the soles,
the souls of the weak, this kind of love is rare and unique...
Death's defeat started with the washing of the feet,
clearing the walkway to eternity's retreat...

Want to Know Why

A son of the damned,
standing in the breach.
No peace with the past,
is within reach...

No trust can be felt,
in the place I stand...
I'm paying the price
of deeds done by my hand...

No silencing this tongue because
this story still has something to teach...
Yes, the past terror still has
it's price to reach...

I'll speak of that which is your shame,
the blood of youth is upon your hands...
It matters not how much you deny,
or the false innocence you command...

It matters not how you've averted your eyes,
the moment of abuse will visit your conscience...
I speak not from vengeance,
begging you to see sense...

These words flow not from
some indescribable mensch,
But from that bruised and battered boy,
you could not see, sitting alone on the bench.

No I'm that strangely quiet girl,
you heard cry, as she hung in the closet to die.
It's the voice of the bent, the broken,
the bullied, and abused by those who hide...

No coach, teacher, preacher, or cop,
ever spoke the truth...
No, they cowered and lied about the marks,
of the black and blue little youth...

When you belittled the deformed,
degrade what you label as "out of the norm,"
You own the terror...
...yet to be born...

No one understands when words of ridicule,
leave the spirit and soul, all torn...
No one stands, with the bullied and forlorn,
carrying the scars that should not be worn ,

To those ignoring what is right,
should carry the scars of scorn to bed each night...
I cheered the day, when you finally stood up,
on that Cleveland bus... it was right.

And when you hear
Natalie sing her song,
it's you who let that shadow,
get that strong...

When the generation of the bullied,
abused and misused do something to confuse,
your lament is always why? why? why...?
The rape, the ravage of abuse,

reaches deeper into the body,
than the light of truth,
The tacit permission to perjure youth,
comes when the teacher neglects the truth.

The marginalized become shooting monsters.
Columbine becomes your unwanted fruit,
When you taught your children to defame,
to shame, in popularity's name,

Pheobe's price is your gain...
I am the voice of the broken and lame,
when you look into the face of pain,
truly you own the price of the unwanted fame...

For when you allow the bullying,
the abuse, the neglect, of youth,
you won't like the results,
but this is the truth...

Morning Shadows

The morning light filters through the lone spruce in the yard,
leaving strangely misshaped shadows to play upon the wall,
Sounds of music, smell of coffee, delay the thoughts of dread,
with no desire to leave the aches of this lumpy bed...

Strugglin' with the thoughts of what broken children we are,
Is there any need for wrecks like me,
Smilin' at the strange shadows play, the sufferin' they symbolize
it troubles them not...

Civilization accepts the devil's comforting keep,
where society sends the sons called the black sheep...
The anguish of bullied broken souls, it comes to call,
the winds of rage, the vengeance of age, comes to call upon all...

Be it suicide or homicide, society denies it's part in all.
Civilized, trivialized, marginalized, compartmentalized,
all responsibility is denied, the blankets of the acceptable
is another lie ...

Like the misshapened shadows on my wall,
darkness gives those sinless sins a place to hide,
To each child's suicide, you cry and cry, your tepid call
to change, a lazy insipid lie...

To each Columbine High you ask, why? why? why?
Your part in the monster play, was when you looked the other way ...
Scars from belts and boards, scores of words that have
cut and torn, leaving a voice that rues the day it was born ...

You will placate and you will buy,
the political hypocrite's cry... why? why? why?
Humanity's wrecks sealed in cages, sit and sigh,
too weary, too broken, and too enraged to try...

Thanking the shadows on the wall, the lights, the darkness,
that comes to call, painting images of nothing at all,
shadows that wander and dance on the wall, hope, desire,
vanish as the shadows do, evaporating like the morning dew,
wondering, as I do, what will be my shadow's due ...

WAR PIG BS.

ABOUT THE AUTHOR

Michael E. Kelley

Michael is serving a life sentence and has been a prisoner for many years. He says that he has survived, to some degree, many prisons such as Lewiston, Turner, & Livermore Falls. For the last twenty years or more, he has been a guest at MCI Cedar Junction [formerly Walpole], Massachusetts.

Although incarcerated, Michael has always written poetry and illustrated numerous religious books and all manner of graphical leaflets and cards, all from his life experiences.

Although denied his liberty, Michael continues to express his profound sense of freedom through his art and poetry.